Mythology of Touch

Other titles by Mary Stone Dockery

Aching Buttons
Dancing Girl Press 2012
dancinggirlpress.com

Blink Finch
Kattywompus Press 2012
kattywompuspress.com

Also from Woodley Press

Begin Again: 150 Kansas Poems
Edited by Caryn Mirriam-Goldberg

Fire Mobile: The Pregnancy Sonnets
by Matthew Porubsky

Kansas Poems of William Stafford
Edited by Denise Low

washburn.edu/reference/woodley-press/

book design by Leah Sewell | leah.sewell@gmail.com

Mythology of Touch

POEMS by

Mary Stone Dockery

Several poems in this collection have been published in the following journals:

Gargoyle, *Red Lightbulbs*, *Thunderclap Press*, *Medulla Review*, *scissors and spackle*, *FutureCycle Poetry*, *The Montucky Review*, *The Adroit Journal*, and *Zaum*. I would like to thank the editors for their support.

I would like to express my indebted gratitude for the guidance and hard work of the many involved in the publication of this collection: Dennis Etzel, Jr., Leah Sewell, Matthew Porubsky, Kevin Rabas, Caryn Miriam-Goldberg, Denise Low, Richard Peabody, Aldon Nielson, and Dr. William Church. For friendship, collaboration, and inspiration, I would also like to thank the members of the Topeka Writers Workshop and the Blue Island Review Writer's Group.

A special thanks to my husband, Dustin, for being there, for listening, for loving. Lastly, I extend my deepest gratitude to my close friends and my wonderful family.

Mary Stone Dockery | dockstone82@gmail.com

for Dustin

introduction

When I teach Mythology, I tell students to dismiss mythologies as "false or unreal stories," but to embrace the stories, per scholars Eva M. Thury and Margaret K. Devinney, as narratives that reflect a perception of the world. This book, Mary Stone Dockery's first published collection of poetry, uses the title Mythology of Touch without coincidence, as each poem enters the visceral plane via the lyrical narrative mode. I also tell my students that we rely on mythology to help us out in our own times of struggle—to search out a means of survival. Finding relationships with others can be that double-edged sword, until we find the means of truly touching and being touched.

Of course, the relationship with a lover—including the lover within—is key to exploring how these mythologies are created. In the title poem, both taxidermy and astronomy are the vehicles the speaker explores the Beloved with:

> We touch through glass
>
> in a mirage of fingertips, ruby
> lines in our palms light exploding
>
> supernovas, purpling dust.

This gentle interweaving of examination—both downward and small, and upward and huge—shapes how a relationship becomes, too. What amazes me about this poem, and how many of the poems work in this collection, is the effortlessness of the metaphor creation: how the metaphors continue and develop:

> the wings of your mouth
> quiver, reshaping words
>
> into clusters of new phrases,
>   formations I can see expanding
> but can't hear, can't touch.

The essence of this poem's examination concludes with language itself—the final metaphor that matches the form: the poem.

The prose poem is another form this collection takes—that elusive form poetics still tries to define since Baudelaire's declaration of the "new poem" in the mid-1850s. However, the prose poetry in this collection needs no definition to be powerful. They seem the natural form in what the mythology behind each is conveying. An example is in the first poem here, "Josh's Flowers":

> You ruined Josh's flowers and now you ache with the sweat of summer, wanting to whip the petals into a stain-glass wind, pull them from the sidewalk, listen to them rub against one another as if one petal was a palm and another a thigh, point them to the weak stalks you tore them from, the stems that had

already begun to droop on the dining room table, and show them how to curl into themselves as petals should, huddling against the cool air conditioned room.

Even if one misses the lyrical style of capturing the mood of the story within one sentence, the reader experiences the narrative's tenor through the vehicle of the flowers and their placement. There is serious gardening that occurs for our reading pleasure—that plants us into these works.

Wherever there is a connection, there is a danger present, and Mary's poetry, too, work within these dangers:

You couldn't hold up
one pen to write down
what had happened.
We knew that the etchings
on the wall were from before -
these carvings of mythology
you copied onto your skin -
from a time when catching
tornadoes and naming them
had been your obsession.
("Tornado Elegy")

Within these true dangers are the loss—the elegiac voice throughout these pieces. Throughout these elegies, there is, nevertheless, a sense of hope and connection—maybe the true nature of the elegy? As a thankful reader, I can't help but to imagine how these poems are of survival:

You sing. You write poems.
...You cut your hair,
paste it to a card for me to
carry in my wallet, and again
we are holding each other
without even touching
("Self-Portrait as Affair")

This collection shows us how the mythology of touch includes the spaces in between—both physical and emotional—and how we both survive and rely on them. The dangers and risks each speaker survives draws us in for a safe haven of our own yearning.

These poems are heartbreaking and beautiful—as well as real. We rely on mythologies to help us survive the traumas and pitfalls of life, and I'm truly happy that this collection is one I can rely on. Thank you, Mary, for sharing.

Dennis Etzel Jr.
Woodley Press
Feb. 2012

contents

Mythology of Touch

1

The Current of Leaving

Josh's Flowers

You ruined Josh's flowers and now you ache with the sweat of summer, wanting to whip the petals into a stained-glass wind, pull them from the sidewalk, listen to them rub against one another as if one petal was a palm and another a thigh, point them to the weak stalks you tore them from, the stems that had already begun to droop on the dining room table, and show them how to curl into themselves as petals should, huddling against the cool air conditioned room.

But it's not going to happen because Josh saw you break the vase against the wall and eat a piece of glass, watched you bleed against the white painted wall while the vase water dripped, forming a grey shadow shaped like a cathedral, dried blood flaking at its door.

After he saw it all, he ran away into the woods behind the house and you could hear him panting out there as if he had never moved in all his life. You imagined his arms as heavy as the petals now trailing from the door to the porch and beyond, out to the mailbox, heavy petals beating into the gravel. It all reminded you of sweat and skin and church pews, wooden, sticking to the back of your thighs in summer.

Josh's flowers had come to you in a package. A clear wrapping protected them. There was a card with a stranger's handwriting. A woman had written it, you could tell, by the curves of the 'y' in 'you' and how the 'I' slanted just so, as if it shimmered in light, as if it might slide into an 'e' or another letter, moving itself into a vowel because of the heat, like a body's slickness, holy and obscene.

And then the light bulb popped in the front room. Sparks on the table. The smell of black. A silhouette came out of the light bulb and stood behind you and kept making you look at the flowers. They were like any other flower ever, red and yellow and pink and orange. Your favorite part was the green leaves exploding from the stems like arms. The flowers seemed to be children asking you to lift them. You imagined them tasting salty, like the sweat of a hand, the petals soft in your mouth, tongues and tongues.

Behind you, the silhouette moved. It wasn't your fault. The flowers were crying in the vase with their green arms, hanging over the lip of the vase as if crawling from a mouth, the wetness rich with a communion of bodies. The green reached and reached.

He would return. Josh would come back to repaint the wall and use a paring knife to harvest glass shards from your teeth. Josh might remain in the woods until he finds a patch of flowers to lie on. Or until he finds clovers, eats them, and feels all new again, like last summer when he showed you how to skip rocks against rocks instead of water. But he would return.

You sit on the porch, your tongue scorching against itself and glass shavings, and you wish to kneel upon such splinters before Josh, to have Josh remember what it's like to be inside of you. The wind rinses the petals with an invisible stain, each sharp glow of red or yellow on the sidewalk in front of you twisting as if pieces of blown glass, the shadows gone, and only now the scent of Josh's flowers, of lilac and ginger, of Josh draining the bathtub, of charred wood and singed fingernail clippings and marble gravestones breaking with age.

As Young as You Remember

Do you have a thing for redheads? she asks, after she has you kiss her in the car, after she tells you the kiss was good, and it is now you realize the flash of red behind you, the hair strands left on your pillow case. The backs of heads were petals bursting out in ruby, glistening in the wine-glow of your bedroom light. Bourbon wrung wisps in your nostrils, against your shoulder. The bourgeoning fibers spill across your past. Her hair, caramel red and cut to her chin, is like a silk scarf in front of you, waiting. How it catches in the wind. You inhale red wherever you find it, touch it to your cheek. She catches you staring at her hair, forgets about your age, your hands wrinkling, forgets about the decay in your fingernails. You know you were fucking your ex-wife the day she was born, on a soft rug in the front room, candles surrounding you, orange cream and cherry blossom. Everything is covered in the smell of blue now. The wife's face is a torturous grin, crinkled into you like a thistled shadow. She is not your wife, not as you had left her. Only cigarettes know how old you are. And coffee stains in the back room. She will never know your mother has hair red as rum and always smelled like violets. She tucks her panties underneath your futon and lies there in a shirt that you know matches. It goes with red. She inhales your second-hand smoke, coos when you read your poems, her fingernails unable to tap at meaning, and tap tap tap is how she listens when she leans against the headboard, mumbles something about Zen. She is as young as you remember them all to be, as young as it can get. Every time you look at her you hope for many more whiskey moments like these, for red hair piling at your door step. You will swirl the strands against the shower wall, wipe them onto your body with a used towel. She looks at you like she has an orchid for a tongue. You have memorized each peak and highlight on her head as if it was blood in your wrist.

To Eat All the Colors

We are the kind of people who drown every day to say we have drowned. It's like eating water with a fork when you look up at me, your face pulled into a scowl, asking my hand to reach for it and smooth it back up your cheeks, as if you did not spend the last thirty minutes splashing, as if you have not drowned at all.

You jump so high you can reach a cloud and pull it down for me with your fingernail. It tastes like gauze when we eat it.

We like dark, dim lights ladling over us.

We make love against cool walls, our thighs scraping with splinters, our backs chipping paint. We peel paint off each other. Pieces spread with sweat. We are always hooked into each other or pulling away from each other, trying to eat all the colors.

We forget to bake the cookies after mixing up the batter and it all just sits on the counter not baking, the oven preheated, the scent of scolding emptying us into separate rooms. Eventually you will smear a handful of cookie mix and chocolate chips on my cheek and I will ask you to drown against me tomorrow, in a silk shower, our feet slipping over baby oil, your hands swirling over me like fans.

Gardening

We are covering our faces because the sun feels like a hot oil lamp against our cheeks. We can't let the sun scorch our skin like last year, when we both had sunglass-shaped burn-lines, our noses so red we could see the tips when we looked down, red and charred, each sniff a scrape of ache, risking burns to other places on our bodies. Red pain like grief. The sun is in mourning and takes it out on us, especially in July when we want to be outside the most to check the peaches and cream corn's growth and pull ragweed and witchgrass along the path to the garden. Corn on the cob is our summer treat, a sign that it's eighty days into summer. The air hot and peppery.

In a few months we will wear hats and pick pumpkins on cool mornings, our arms wet with dew. But for now, we stand next to each other in a small lump of soil, waiting for a breeze to break into us, to flash, to burst against us sudden and cool. Your fingernails have dirt crusted beneath them. My fingernails are chipping again. The smell of soil on our gloves and around us, dirt, the beginning of things, right beneath our feet, and still we cover our faces, a lazy buffer between the sun and ourselves, the hot-glow of the river. Mosquitoes are like lightning bolts flaring up and out from the dampness, barreling at us and flying off to die again like we wish sometimes we could. Your skin has more colors than morning and you flash in front of me as if you reflect the crisp chlorine water of a pool, but no, you are just flickering before me, the sun so hot it thaws the colors of you into a swirl, asks them to burst and explode around you till they drip, dissolve, soften.

I am fine with us standing here covering our faces but I want to kiss you in the soil, to pull you to the ground and press my lips to the layer of dirt on your cheek, touch the dust on your kneecaps, gulp the sultry scent of crabgrass, violets, and other weeds. You are looking away, though, into the haze. You are reddening again. Pink for now, the color of a flower you once gave me or the color of a bead on a necklace, yet the edges are crisp, blooding as we stand, but tomorrow I will rub aloe on your legs and arms, my fingers will suction to your body and we'll laugh and our faces will still be white, clean, soft as the green of the leaves we walk on, red churning in the distance.

Fixed Inside

I stay home these days because the numbness fills me, reaches inside my fingertips and blows as if it's trying to anesthetize my hands from the inside out. If I reach for you, you might see how each vein bulges blue and grey, and we could imagine together the insides of my hands, where red traces into the pinks of flesh or into the blackness of the sores we would uncover, into the oozing, and you would immediately know my hands needed to be held. Just from seeing them from the inside. Instead, the meds creep along in there, working dull colors into me like haunting scents. Violet mostly, the smell of old candle wicks that can no longer light. Or the scent of gauze, grey. I wake to limbs hurting with the loss of circulation, deadened, thick. Every time you grab an arm you don't recognize on your bed or beneath your pillow, its contours unfamiliar, soft, it will haunt you. I do this every day and you say that there is an outside where the sky changes colors or where the grass smells like children's feet. You say things are different out there. And I think, Or they aren't. Inside, I can sense my toes and know they exist but only because my hypochondria allows me to believe they will turn black and break off like pieces of ice, then bob in the tub water. I must stay here, inside, sleeping, wrapped in soft quilts, where I can touch my skin with my own hands, where the only thing that stuns is sunlight clawing through a moved curtain. Or darkness rubbing against my leg like a cat. Wrapped here, softened, I am fixed inside the unfeeling. The silverware gleams, but within its drawer, you say. At least it gleams.

Too Much to Drink

Tequila is a broken riddle entering me and it drills against my temples in hot beats. Yes. No. I can't remember. Don't. My drink ends up sloshing on your suit vest. Fuck off. Your purple tie zigzags in the light. Later, at dinner parties, we will joke about me biting the door man's arm when he reaches to drag me out. Suck it. I will wake up tomorrow remembering my body in the air, heavy, fuck you, how they carried me in my new dress all hands against lace, fingers pressed into my back, my kidney swollen inside of me, I told you this would happen, my tights tearing, that bitch better get out of the way. Tossed into snow. Fuck. The wind that night is the sharpest memory. Sobering. I hate you. My high heels have drink stains. You never listen and I hate you again. My wrists and arms already yellow-green bruises. Fuck you. What did you say? We yell on the car ride home, you suck, you don't even see me, did you think I looked pretty, and I pound my fist against the glove box. The tequila swelters inside me like a hot knife, it razors my esophagus, pull over so I can throw up, pull over so we can fuck, it's so cold, where's my coat, and I want to make love to you but how do I say it? At some point I will pee outside again and again our marriage has turned into a couch marathon, a game to see who can touch less.

Every House on Our Street Has a Baby in It

Except mine. That makes twelve babies and one more on the way because Regina or Robin is about to have her second one, which means all the other moms on the street will soon walk around with their pregnant slippers on. They all have babies together and to celebrate they wear cartoon character slippers, Bugs and Donald and Jack the Pumpkin King. Fluffy heads scrape asphalt as soon as the weather changes. The bigger, more animated the slipper, the happier the mom and child.

The babies do not stay hidden in their happy houses. They come out in strollers and wear big bows. Mike and Jeannie's baby always has a giant red flower on her forehead. I always wish to tell them this is ridiculous. You can't see the baby's whole face. The elastic band leaves crinkles in the baby's soft skin reminding me of raw hamburger, the way the baby skin worms and wrinkles beneath it.

The man I live with – who is not yet my husband and very well may never be– refuses to look at the babies when we are out walking. He looks at the sky and nods his head and does not let any part of any baby touch him. Instead, I have to look, coo, and imagine the babies are plastic or silicone, like those real dolls I've seen on television.

One baby has cheeks that remind me of marshmallows expanding in a vacuum container – his cheeks are fatter each time I see him. Everything about the baby reminds me of food. His arms are cream puffs stuffed into baby clothes. His legs are rounds of white cheese. His tummy, engorged as if he has swallowed another baby, a loaf of homemade bread. Every time I leave him, I find myself standing in the kitchen eating a whole block of mild cheddar and

a frozen pizza. Unconsciously, the man who is not yet my husband says, I must want to eat babies. He always makes jokes about eating babies or poking them with pitch forks. I do my best not to laugh.
The mothers leave notes on my porch. They say things like, "Stick in there!" and "Soon you'll know love like we do." They put pictures of the babies in envelopes and leave them on my porch. I would have more pictures of babies than anyone would know what to do with, but I don't keep them because it's like I can smell baby all over the house every time I open the envelope – a diaper seems to hover in the corner, or a wet burp towel lies over my shoulder. I spread the pictures out on the living room floor when I get them, look at how the babies smile with their baby eyes. Imagine the smell of baby on my sleeves. Hear babies burp and cry. The crying lasts a long time. When I have imagined the babies and the crying and the tiny baby shoes, I light matches and watch each photo burn down to my finger, the photo blackened, curling, and finally disappearing into piles of ash on the carpet.

Gone – the baby with the fat cheeks in the Tigger costume. Gone – the baby wrapped in red velvet, sitting on Santa's lap, red-faced and crying. Gone- the babies in wheel barrows and sleds and wagons. Gone - the baby skin that reminds me of Grandma's peanut butter fudge. Gone - the babies in candy cane dresses. Gone - the fat cheeks and big heads. Every cliché baby - gone.

I sprinkle the ashes out my window onto the flower bed. Not because it helps flowers grow but because I don't know what else to do with the ashes and it seems like throwing it all in the trash can would somehow be such a waste.

This is What Pain Looks Like

A wet petal flung against a wall. It sticks there, dries. Presses itself into the wall like a fossil. When you try to scratch it off with your fingernail, it has become part of the wall. No matter how hard you try, the petal, though once thin and blowing in wind, has turned itself into drywall and it prefers synthetic, hard. It cannot imagine being pressed in a book and crumbling in soft hands.

Or this is what pain can look like when you forget what flowers are. When we forget where to look for the scents we crave and instead vinegar fills the room. Or pain is only a white piece of paper or the paper cutting you or you crumbling paper because you have nothing to say, and the flowers have never even existed.

It is nothing, not even the hospital room cabinets filled with cards. The cards in black trash bags are not pain. Pain acts like a chair. It sits there. You sit on it. We all move it around the room to make more space.

A question in your throat when you haven't had enough sleep. It's a repeat, a movie you've seen too many times, the sound of pennies shaking in an aluminum can. Your ears are. Listening. You are busy pressing more wet petals into the wall. Talking about painting over them. How what pain looks like is the new interior fashion. Dead flowers and black paint and your fingernail bleeding splinters.

Almond Milk and Rosemary

He was a baby throwing a tantrum again, and she had not seen it in pictures, had not been warned how blue his cries would sound. Because of him she left her hymen on a doorstep, where it shriveled, twisting blue-black and purple, an orchid spraining against the cold, and she finally forgot what it looked like.

She had forgotten about her legs, her need for them, for seeing a moment and walking toward it, for peeling it from the horizon and hanging it on her body, a sheet of bourbon-skimmed lines, the fabric of emery boards, all wish and whine bleeding against her. For standing up and taking what had once been hers. She had forgotten it completely, and yearned for it, for flexibility, elasticity, for caress and caress.

What was it anyway? It was another blue bird perched on its marble bath in the backyard then flying away when she whispered its name. It was another Bob Marley lookalike chaffing his fingers up her thighs and into her, saying, Redemption. It was another bug smashed against a windshield, splattering, oozing across glass, its blackness etching along her ribs, or was that her lung revealed, her kidney, her liver? Was it her body turning itself inside out, exposing her insides, what she lacked? There he was again, naked before her, always naked, fists blanking the screen, bees swirling invisible around the two of them, the sound of bees prickling in her teeth.

His fingernails were turning black again, his silhouette flashing canary.

She held a pretend camera in her hands. She told him she pictured herself as the lip of a yellow world. She longed to be written, to be loved in a smattering of words. She wanted to be a bathroom stall door, with its numbers and jagged letters, its hate. Her hands altered each squared space before her, somehow right beneath her thumb nail. Pill scratches and oiled prisms, her pictures all made of his scribbled lies. She knew how to accidentally magnify wrinkles or find creases in hidden skin. He stood over her, smelling of almond milk and rosemary, and she realized she hadn't paid attention to her own hands, reminding her how it would forget about her, and over and over it did, as her arms swirled in front of her, reminding him of chiffon ribbons and silk, peach and blurring reds, until while he watched, he could no longer find her face in the cloud of skin, until her moans pushed against both of them, heavy as shadows.

Essay on Electricity

A finger touches a door handle. A finger is a match. There is no flame, only heat, spark, push. Glass powder in the air. When the windows ache with leaving, his fingernails scrape panes. Looking for callous, for face. The pain entered through the walls soaked in gasoline. Scars shivered with light, as if on fire. It was about pleasing you. Him. Sectioning off pieces of hair to stick to walls. The voltage of each hair strand moon orchid scent clinging to sheets. A lack of oxygen makes it celestial, the inside of a black hole, the unknown, his fist. Gravity waves spilling in colors from one mouth to another in black and silver, lips the same silky substance of clouds. Placed next to a window like a flower, bodies might wilt, instead we bloom into the sky blushing. The friction. If he was believed, he might return. The current of his leaving shadow-burned and sulfurous, striking the hard surface-grit in my teeth.

Spinning

She was dreaming of motorcycles again and riding them over and over on a blackened road, the tires all scorched spinning, tugging her to the sound of the ocean states and states away. It was always like that, her tongue a corpse in her mouth, the handlebars pushing against her palms like hard whispers. She was silent, spinning. Trees extended their green leaves, nothing more than hands of ghosts, their branches a tangle of arms and gloom and reach. She was used to the sound of cicadas when the roads narrowed, how their drone exploded around her then lifted, the murmur of the world just like a soft breeze right when you need one. She rode through the Ozarks and their weary bluffs, through sands and cacti and clouds. Dusk and its rum-glow of light. Maps she had memorized were grime inside her, yellow lines and stitches, other worlds leather-spun. Who needed a watch? Who needed to know what time it was when the whispers of insects and the hum of the road vibrated through you? Who needed anything other than the scent of leather, the jingle of a demon bell? Her father had given her the bell with its notched silver, the winged edges of an angel opening up to catch ghosts of the road. Every ring, every rattle, told her shadowed spirits were veils dropping to blacktop gusting behind her, and she imagined them in her wake, clawing her back tire, willing a soft edge of road to push her down, a skid, a slide. There would be hundreds of them behind her, a swirl of shadow and smoke like hurricane waves curling up to catch her. She imagined their phantom-claws sprinkled with road rash, their cries the sound of chrome crunching against earth. She couldn't speak back, couldn't do anything but agree with the methodical hum of nature around her and breathe the throb and tremble of the bike, press it harder against her, let the wind scrape her face, the wind opening and closing like scissors before her. She would ride all the way to the ocean, then turn around and come back, her tires spinning with salt and foam, and she would continue to ride right through the shudder of blossoming sunsets, through each pulsing beat of splintered horizon.

2

How to Erase the Dead

How to Erase the Dead

Grab the cracked whiskey bottle,
let its contents leak, sweet, into
your palm. Lick the drops,
warm on your tongue. Use
this same tongue to describe
the roads back home as gravel-spun,
as rising, as flesh-like whispers,
dust. Palms and broken glass,
windshields shattered
before dawn. The roads
are the same color as your tongue –
pomegranate and honey,
a swirl of fog and mirage, dewy
with the breath of maps.
Trace the squiggly lines, the cut-off
borders with your tongue, bleed
purple-red stain into corners
of wrinkled and aging paper
your smooth palm skin.
Hold the whole place inside
your mouth, shift it around,
wetting it like a small stone.
Here is the gloss: the smear
of your mother's shoulder
lost in folds of paper,
silhouette of a small child
vinegar soaked, fading colors.
Taste the rust and tarnish.
Your tongue numbs itself
beneath the whiskey, scratches

against edge of glass in hurried
cuts, a dried leaf tongue,
just to cut, to empty,
dehydrate. Reach for the map
key and its symbols, for
north or south, looking for faces
whiskey-spun and splotched
far beyond the center.
You will find it, somehow after
erasing it, sealing in a scent
of violets, tombstone, and ash.

Letter for What We Did That Summer

We took turns strangling each other,
because it was what teens did then.
First you pushed me against the wall
by my neck until a darkness arrived
in numbing waves – when I dropped
you watched the twitches of my body
and stood silent, waiting for it to end.
It only took a few minutes for your hands
to seal the shadows into me, for things
to happen. Once, I dreamt your hand
ladling light over me like gravy, a smile
swinging above me in long arcs of white,
moons everywhere, blinking off and on.
Another time, it was as if I had spent
an entire afternoon in bed with you
watching each other above the covers
touching our bodies. The numbness
was arousal, deep, inviting. I dreamt
of filling spaces on the bed with wax,
to mold body parts, curves of you
for later, notching crescents in your skin
with my fingernails – somehow I knew
you would leave, even in the soft
moments when my body convulsed
before you as if waving good-bye,
and when I woke, you pulled me up
by my arms, turned to face me,
and in my eagerness, I was quick
to reach out to you and choke you back.

Greeting Card in a Missouri Accent

You have always been bluffs
like green smoke in the distance

I view you from a highway placed
on top of hills as if a tongue, swelling
toward you in rolls and the letters
s and r, in curves and whispers.
The way you open to the land, erotic.
In winter, your colors break and bend
beneath ice, searching. Green becomes
memory. Yet you stretch anyway.

When I first saw you, I knew I would
not miss you. And I don't. Not from
the side of a road with my thumb
pushed out to cars. Not from the edge
of trees lining the coil of your body,
where I once put my hands. I misuse
the word restore, as though it is
an act of simplicity, not magic. Nothing
remains of the burned barns. The flood
took the house with it. We stare at ground,
imagining stairs to a bedroom with trees.
Restore: That which cannot happen
without deteriorate. Wheat fields
burn and so you burn, too, keeping
what the gardens keep. I watch,
chewing seeds, thanking you across
the green, hesitantly, for the lack of storm.

Tornado Elegy

We arrived to find the gold-
rimmed lids opened beneath
the bed; your hands tornado-
spun, green, your strength,
a scent of gunmetal and orchid,
eroded – rotating above
the headboard, visible and blue.
You couldn't hold up
one pen to write down
what had happened.
We knew that the etchings
on the wall were from before –
these carvings of mythology
you copied onto your skin –
from a time when catching
tornadoes and naming them
had been your obsession.
We found labels peeled
and cut into pieces tossed
by the bed. How temporary
and weak your sky
had become, these fragments
of blue and gray. You picked
at scars scraped and bleeding
across the walls of your skin,
shaved with tails of
tornadoes. Turning, your face
blackened before us. We looked
out the broken window
imagining tornadoes fleeing
like butterflies emptied
from brittle golden cages.

Letter for What I Thought Before

Let me build it for you: the silo's brick walls,
acres of golden wheat, levies of steel and soil,
crumble and tarnish of a grain elevator, corn
stalks brittle as September leaves. When I build –
each wrinkle of a tree trunk, sounds of timber
and gravel road crunching beneath tractor tires
find your palms and fill you, soothing us
deep, eroding. It felt good before, realizing
how small we were in the seed truck,
            our arms folding and unfolding
as we swam in soybeans. To walk along your
your road is to hope it might wrap over me oil-black,
the scent of gasoline, contraband of harvest, rock
and ragweed, the things of this farm, your hands
beneath a water faucet, blackening the white bowl,
tattooed oil in grooves of palms. I could pretend
you saw only me   from the mile marker, even
as I became part of the muddy Missouri overtaking
a driveway, then shadow-thin, a tick in the dust
                                        and ache of road.

*

I would change before you many times.
Unfiltered light, skin, softening windows.
That is the comfort of settling: thinking
gasoline will protect from sunburn, that its oil
and slickness will haunt only in scent. I have
a whole life to watch my skin blister and wrinkle
with age, to be fucked in white silence.
                                        You were a crop
I could not stop to gather. Sometimes I wonder

if there were ever shadows big enough to hide
the wooden chest we built and filled as children
then stuck high up on a rafter of a wilting barn,
if it will be there long enough to disappear
along the torn levee – another wet wound
opening toward us.

Letter After Admittance

When we last saw each other,
the sky was a blue pillow pressing
against the earth. I might have
touched it. Your hand had woven
into the parasol's handle. You
carried it like a cane, refusing
to open it, your sky.
You didn't want anything to fall.
Much later I could finally
lift you onto the bed myself
your bloody fingertips gone.
You said to pause, to wait for the mail
to arrive with the box of news stories,
fingernails, eyelashes, things you kept
sending until they came back again
with your name all over the box,
yellow, black. Wet. Slick, your name
in hurried slurs and curves.
You tied rosaries to your hair,
called them your dreams. You must
remember the last time sky domed
toward us, warped and blue, heavy
as I imagine you now in the hospital
breathing with bandages

Before the Elegy

I wanted him gone: bones
like whispers beneath dirt,
trembling and silent.
Hadn't I given him enough
to suture his self-inflicted cuts?
The thread disintegrated
beneath his touch. We ate
glass together, just to feel
shards of deceit against
the tongue. The language
that cuts speak, blood
and bitter. This is what
I took from him - cynicism
the shape of a knife.
He hid beneath counters,
beds, couch cushions, pulling
me onto his lap in the weak
hours of afternoon. I took
him like he took me, silent
and filled with edges, our bodies
glass sheets in bed. He was always
looking outside, watching for birds,
for sunsets streaked in gloss,
not realizing the dusk from fire.
We breathed enamel toward curtains,
hoping jewels would drop
into our palms after:
when we knew change
had arrived in polishes, gleaming
with sharpened knives

Letter After Making Love

Sometimes when I orgasm
I consider the outside world
at that very moment, its
        curves of sky, edges
of wet swamps, how fast
each car really travels, rubber-
echo abrasions on asphalt,
        the way my arms look
draped over someone else's,
pink, separate. It's as if everything
separates, moving in red-green
        flashes against the outside
of the building - we can even
hear air hiss from floor vents,
movement open and swift,
        our legs and our skin nothing
more than costumes -
        gold trim, polish
and we are glistening

Letter for the Last Time I Saw You

Let me redraw the steps to the back porch
of that half-built house where you point

one finger to the sky, searching for a star
trail we swore was close enough to hear –

steel guitars moaning in night sky. Another
paint-by-number, we colored our atmosphere

in aluminum and blown glass. The sweat
of a beer can stickying to our hands, fresh.

Your chosen color – red, for the cardinals.
Mine – blue, and glittering. I liked to mirage

beneath the street lamp, wavering. You once
put your hand through me and we shuddered

within the translucence, you poked around
for the sound of stars inside of me, wind chimes,

bitter wings, golden, glass. Later, lying
on top of the car, you claimed to know many

constellations but could name none.
You drew my birthday in the sky with a finger,

scraping at black with fingernails, etching
another trail, heads of Gemini, hooves of Taurus,

months stretching over us, expanding, empty.
We made wishes upon one another

with our mouths, tracing seams along skin
to find later, hoping to open again

in bright colors, to find our numbers,
the patterns of our many skins, these
lines now stained, now sealed.

Within the Elegy

His leaving - needles along my cheekbones,
where his finger had touched only hours earlier.
It was as if his tongue still moved across my eyebrows,
ghost of movement on my skin, this dreaming over me,
his shadows, his shadow hands. He had stipulated:
Wear me on you wherever you go, like a coat
or another scarred skin. His words were broken flowers,
petals dying and crackling beneath feet, reminders
of his flesh. The shape of his hand molded
into my side. He lived within a frame on the wall,
poised and debonair, watching. That's when I noticed
the color of his skin changing in the photo,
creases forming in the old paper, the yellow and brown
edges, his teeth blackening before me. His whispers
ink-like and heavy, wrote over me. He wanted me
to remember what it was like to be moved,
and I felt his mouth as if from another room
                    crossing reveries like oceans to get to me.

Letter After Separation

In the city I found
a sidewalk cluttered
with walkers, an open
ballroom of concrete
and leather shoes, scraping.
Heels striking. Motivated
            and haunted.
Disarming. The buildings
tinted the street in cobalt.
I can't remember the faces.
Only that when I stepped
from one side of the street
to the next, my foot dragged
along the tincture of breath,
the scent of iodine, blood,
rust. The dancers unglued
from the set. It only took
a moment for me to look up,
to see no one I knew,
for the air to heave
against me again, for my body
to convulse as if
with dream, with knowing.

What It Means When He's Away

In dreams he is stirring, coiled
over the bodies of other woman.
I wake to the kind of fuck yous muttered
in a hot shower, alone. Mornings, I peel
a banana and his face warps each age spot,
graying. I'll ingest that, too. A sidewalk
becomes his back. I remember looking
at it in soft light, his back stretching over
a bed as if for weeks. Concrete-edged,
he breaks open fruit, places apples
and oranges on dressers, nightstands,
book shelves. In other dreams,
the fruit has rotted, molded into a black
bloom opening toward air filled
with something I'm unable to name.
Mornings become gloom-filled, thick.
Instead of checking his messages
searching for proof with jealousy
hot in my mouth, its deep cuts,
I watch him sleep. I'll move his hand
when he holds himself inside his boxers
for too long. Check to see how close
the moles are on his back, if they've moved,
if his skin stretches with guilt. Over breakfast,
I tell him how often he's cheated -
We laugh so quickly. I want a thick kiss
to prove he smells like himself.
There are pockets in my sleep filled
with something like what it means
when he's away, like what I'll never know –

This deepness in me that somehow thinks
 it knows, gives it his face, the curve of his body,
his dark voice. When the day ends,
I go to sleep wanting to touch him
but I don't let myself ask.

My Insomnia

We hold hands beneath
the table, rub palms,
touch just to touch, to feel
mesh and plead of body,
the blink that lies beyond
sleep. It works its ghost
hands into me, prodding
shadows into skin.
I can't stand up alone
without this support,
without knowing there
is nothing waiting for me
in the softness of my bed.
It is the nothingness
my body craves, the corpse-
like movement, emotion,
bone-brittle words
haze and bleed of
numb, of this,
of lack.

All Saints Day 2011

For Robin

November's dead leaves
lie beneath a too-warm sun
no longer moving, scent
of dust remnants cling
to lungs. The poison
works itself into the ground
like winter does. Pulling
things in with it – your body,
the curve of a casket, roses,
crumpled letters, burned edges.
Mostly when I think of you
it's now, when the leaves
act like the teeth in your mouth,
dried and crusted, falling
in weeping syllables to the ground.
It's the smell of them
that reminds me of the skin
on your shins and palms,
like wings of a moth crusted
and dead on the front porch.
Instead of leaving, I stay
and watch the tree before me
its limbs, its crying. I remember
the ice falling from trees like
this one, in angry thrusts
last winter, crashing through
our front door. I say
"our" but you were only there
in a frame on a wall, sitting
next to an oak tree. Your hair redder
than I'd ever seen, as if

you'd always appeared that way,
smiling, hands folded on your lap,
as if you'd never faded into the lines
of my face and stayed. Your hands
were folded in front of you,
palms pressed together like frozen leaves
when I saw you last – August,
but I remember it as November,
as empty holidays spent in static
and sweaters. You are there
holding a flower pot in your hands,
one you painted yourself.
Or is it a wood carving of a bear
or a rosary that you hold,
keeping your hands
from touching each other,
from reaching out to touch me
as I forever wrestle a rake
against a frozen ground in our front yard,
the scrape and crack of piling leaves.

Letter for Physicality

I cry *My body*
and the buildings
warp against sky
shiver-metal
mirage
of city, of hands.
It grows dark
and darker.   Still.
Each breath
a small amnesia,
the tender
wing of desire
droops into
a Scotch glass.
Disintegrates
inside my mouth.
To ghost myself
along the seams
of this story, our
frames, broken
glass. The empty
of it all. The way
you forget to touch
the body I can't
find in shadows.
My ring finger
swollen in this humidity,
my body another
slurred memory
empty road

of smudged silhouettes.
We are the city,
blackened doors,
the gently forgotten.

After Getting the Mole Removed

We ate hard peaches, wishing we had
picked up the other ones.

These were more like pears, you said,
hard, missing that peach juice.

We ignored the bandage on your left hand,
the shadow of dried blood

that shone through. I imagined the black
mole, scraped off a scalpel

into a clear jar. After, you had to stock up
on sun-block and left-handed gloves.

The doctor would be going over each mole
one by one in the exam room,

every few months; I vowed
to get to them before anyone else –

to linger over them with my breath,
to brush them with the care I would a nipple.

I didn't tell you how it had looked like
the stigma of a flower, how I couldn't

help but wonder if each mole on your pale skin
was made up of a cluster of smaller moles,

if these buds could fall, scatter along
your limbs and make others grow.

I didn't know what pollinated them,
the sun or the touch of my hand.

After the Elegy

Vinegar collected in his bones
a memorial on my windowsill,
where he had once sat watching
the birds. Every piece of furniture
smelled like his skin, sweet
and raw. The carpet
was a callus I walked on.
Hadn't I wanted him gone?
And still, the house created
a lack of him I had never
felt before – coffee mug rim
the shape of his bottom lip,
a warm shower, his fingers
pressing and pressing, his eyes
in a broken light bulb
engraving my finger
in nicks. Everywhere
they had said, I would find
parts of him, even his voice
a sever, an ache, the thump
of a belt in the dryer,
as it spun cycles of heat -
his pelvis against mine,
        the slashing curves
between orgasms -
his breath resides there
a haunt of swell and sweat.

3

The Self-Portraits

Poem for Your Early Twenties

Nights in bars,
sweat on backs, blurred
dancing on the table in flip-flops
for free shots and a few Camels
forgetting the water bill and groceries
numbers written on pieces of scrap
paper, the crumpled clothes
in the morning, stealing
twenty dollars after fucking
someone you just met
then getting out of there
while he showers, the cops
pulling you over once, twice
so many times you only recall
a fear of black and white
chain-smoking
learning to use the word fuck
remembering that guy's lack
of chest hair, but not his name,
waking up in jail on your period,
waking up in jail enough times
to lose count, waking up
on a staircase a used condom
next to your head, a cat watching
the judge saying you look too
innocent for disorderly conduct
poker, bad karaoke, martinis
pissing on someone's porch
because he's cheating
no one will be your boyfriend

go all day without eating
because all your money goes
to tipping the bartender, free
drinks,   up all night till seven
in the morning, fucking
Chad on the pool table at the bar
after hours, just to say you've
done it, driving home so messed
up your windshield swirling
burns with dew, waking up
cotton mouthed, hazy, tense
always, it seems, you wake up
            to touch a headache
re-learning the meaning of fuck
pissing behind the bar at Muny Inn
men are always watching you
            take off your pants
needing the kind of massage
that could reach to that warm
place inside you keep hidden
            running out of cigarettes
all the men in your bed and gone
the next day and watching Lifetime
drunk by yourself just to cry
being so bored with life
you masturbate every day
before you leave the house
play lonely songs on repeat
            pretend you remember
cuts from broken beer bottles

scars, bruised hickeys,
dating a guy you don't even like
because he buys the alcohol
feeds you in the morning
writing when you can
age burning through you
nothing in your wake
but Vodka and ash.

The Abortion

It wasn't on a blanket
in San Diego, wind breeching
the yard in scarred torrents,

your breath working
onto my collarbone,
my back pressed against rocks,
the smell of snails, bushes, tumbleweeds.

It wasn't the story you told me
on a bus ride to the city,
your hand against my hip, you pull me

in and pull me
in, tell me how your grandmother
made applesauce at home,

using a peeler her mother
and mother's mother had used,
how she would pile

cinnamon on top of apple mush, stirring
long into her days,
the kitchen apple scented, wrinkles
on her hands apple-filled.

When we are not in the Midwest anymore
I can picture your story on paper
the same way I can picture pink
applesauce, buckets and apple peels.

But it wasn't your past and my past
meeting at a bus stop, the corner
of Broadmore and Crest,

where our umbrellas touched in the rain,
my pants rolled to my knees.
It wasn't

in the city or near a river. It wasn't
on paper. It wasn't
your mother and I shopping for dresses,

her hand grazing my breast
when I can't zip it up myself.

It wasn't wrapped in pink and red ribbons,
in a box stuffed with Styrofoam,
a silent shake, an apple

on a teacher's desk, a cherry tree.
Of all things, it was not
a cherry tree and you were not there

and I was yet to believe it
and we both forgot about it in May,
with the other weather, when the apples

began to ripen, before we remembered
about apples and their sharp stems,
the blankets and stars, fruit trees

bending in Santa Ana winds,
before we even let it happen,
the scent of lemon peels
forever tossing against air.

The Dream Diary

1.

Last night I dreamed of castles without doors
of helicopters, steering wheels, flight or movement
your smile
                                        hooked in a rearview mirror
a woman's hand covering your eyes, her fingernails
chipping black, another palm cupping your chin.

The moon drifted around me, its long arms sweeping
scent of carcasses.
                                        I woke with sweat lining
my lip, my lower back, the places you will touch

after I tell you it happened again, how you did it
again.

2.

I walk on a roller coaster, its red rails reaching
over a jungle
                                        beyond me only red, sky
like a wound, the rails of the coaster stretch

then I am on the ground again, watching bombs
fall onto houses, running as ash explodes around me

3.

At first, you are not there
and the people I meet know my name, but I don't
know theirs.
You always appear in rooms
where light bulbs have sparked out, the smell of black
like a tongue stickying my lips and fingers

It's here I find another woman in a garter belt

her hands push against your chest
her high heels
scrape your back

You smile at me. I smile back. For some reason
I am not even mad.

4.

There are dogs all over the house.

I am napping, and they rush in the room,
onto the bed, barking in my face
saliva
drizzling over me
like olive oil on a white plate

and I can't move my arms or legs, can't
move a thing

my entire body
paralyzed, half-awake, sleeping in a dream,
unable to wake up in either place, there
or here,   arms steel bars in water.

Later, when my limbs become light again
the walls are still, more white than

they have ever been before,
and you keep   changing the channel.

5.

last night you cheated
again. I wake up knowing you are hiding
from me   a sliver of the moon,
perhaps, the kiss from a soft woman in black,
light bends at your eyes breaking into pieces

there are many options
many things for me to imagine, prisms
and women   dangling from rearview
mirrors. One choice always leads to another.

In my dream you laugh
and women giggle in your ears. Once I even found you
with another man,   and still, you laughed,
the sound heavy as bells, shuddering the floor.

Self-Portrait as Highway

A black tongue
its open curves

bending just for you

sting and skid
of wind, of movement

your weight unpredictable
as water; you write
over me in sweat

until asphalt explodes
burning coal
novas, shrapnel
of burned flesh

beneath you, I move,
as if dissolving -

twist, grind

rocks, like teeth
into skin

Parallels

On the side of glass
with colors you swirl
your hips as if before a mirror
your body in drifts fitted
for someone else's palm
an echo your body
pitches its sighs
toward our doors but there
is no blackening no orchid
bruise blooming a scrape
of vowels, those grazed hums
you sweat you swell your
breath reflects
in soft spots on the glass
you draw circles your fingers
stained abrasions of glass
splinters parallels imitating
body movement smiling
corpses touch fingers
to disappear in colors
of a fingertip smeared glass

Fog

You stand on a terrain of rug, now
a wilt of old cotton, only filament,
its slack shape forgotten,

too many stringing loops to mend,
and even if we wanted to, we are tired,
and hurt from standing so long.

Instead, we want to paint motion
onto discolored borders, hang quilts over windows.
When I refuse to wake in the morning

to sounds of paint cans toppling in the garage,
spatters of merlot and chestnut chalking
across the floor silent, drawing gravel

into grooves, the paint moving
until it finds its walls, and when
I still refuse to wake to the scratch

of unknowns on the hardwood floor,
it is 5 a.m., and you're flying into my arms,
a child unsure, knowing the roof contains

phantoms, dreams of flight. I want
to know where you have come from
with your sudden sadness, your wet arms,

yellow paint dripping from your lip.
You bring the scent of outside – nothing more,

nothing less – the only baptism

our bedroom has yet to consider.
We watch from the windows
as fog droops from the bluffs,

feel the tug of the house,
with its scaffolds and braces,
knowing its soft windows,

its browning light
might compel us
into separate rooms.

Self-Portrait as Affair

We bleed indigo, you are sure
of it.   Still, I'm not finding
your hands here, not anymore,
not since _______. Instead,
I see you on stage making out
with a microphone, palm up
as if pressed to the ceiling.
You are always making out
with something, these days,
a rebel,   reveling
in a newfound heat of
jealousy on your tongue.
You are holding things up,
you say these days. Holding
it in. I watch morphine-clouds
hover over you, lax and waste
of whiskey breathing across
the top of your hand. See,
we don't do it anymore, not
how we used to.   You
wake up with emptiness lit
inside of you, saying, Where
are we now? Have we moved?
There are blood stains
on our sheets, but not from me.
You have always been sure
that grass and heat and August
are the three things we need.
But   August spins
only once a year, burning

and brown and dull. The heat
so pressing that you refuse
to sleep next to me anymore.
You sing. You write poems.
You refuse to pick up a phone,
call your mother, tell her
you can no longer have children,
that you are proudly addicted
to the way light   reflects
through your glass of Vodka.
We let it happen once, you say,
but this time, things will be
different. You cut your hair,
paste it to a card for me to
carry in my wallet, and again
we are holding each other
without even touching

Giving

Night thumped the window pane
when he was born
and they put him into my arms,
a bullet into a chamber.

They had dipped him in copper first,
wrapped him in a steel blanket,
then gave him to me and waited.

He looked up at me for the first time,
with a chin like mine,
a dimple on his right cheek,
the light candling his face.

His mass pushed my abdomen inward,
as I let him curl at my belly
for the last time, coiled
into the springs of my arms.

Silence tumbled around me,
perching on empty shelves
in the hospital room,
opening the quiet for us.

No one brought petunias.
The nurse stood in the doorway
checking her wristwatch.

I grasped the cold rail of the bed,
my arms withdrawn like elastic.
They wheeled him away
while I lay on my side,
feeling something like the moon
as it greened the sky.

Self-Portrait as Woman

Before they came for me, I exfoliated in white wine,
watched the glass empty itself like it had every
time before, watched the way my hands exposed
the blue-red veins beneath the skin, how my
fingers would keep moving, touching buttons
or peeling the label from the bottle, or reach
for an invisible choke in the air, grasp, release
nothing. I had waited a long time for their smiles,
their long arms, white teeth. I had waited a long
time to be held like that in someone's arms,
as if being lifted for the first time. And they took
me, carried me into a place where my body
disappeared slowly into grains of paint, colors
and canvas. There I was able to watch them all,
my hair never blowing up in the wind, the wine
bottle on the table before me never opening,
never spilling, their faces before me large, eerie,
my ability to see more in their pores
                                        than they in me.

Mythology of Touch

You have always been cranberry,
        soft jazz swaying in front of me
your mouth wings of a moth

carcass that dreams itself
across my shoulder blade.

You read books on taxidermy,
        collect crisp bodies of June
bugs, crushing them

to salt your glass for mint juleps.
When you sip, a constellation

of teeth grimaces toward me –
        belts and points of white bone,
all lines. We touch through glass

in a mirage of fingertips, ruby
lines in our palms light exploding

supernovas, purpling dust.
        Yours is an anatomy of mask,
coverings, layers, we are used

to shadows flicking like tongues,
the glass wedged between us

a game, where I imagine
        its slick lines becoming the grit
of your salt, cold knives pressed

against our wounds, glass shaped
like gauze, but it's not a game

you say, it's safe, it's how myths
begin, two bodies moving
together on opposite sides

of a glass slab, stars printing
themselves onto corners, the way

your light reflects through glass
shooting down toward my feet
where it burns, acidic and dry

the wings of your mouth
quiver, reshaping words

into clusters of new phrases,
formations I can see expanding
but can't hear, can't touch.

Self-Portrait as Lovers

                    At the window. A hummingbird. A ghost.
Wings scraping the highway. Like your lips

          across my shoulder blade. The sound of ache.
A stinging whisk. A palpitation of asphalt. Of breath. Sometimes
                    I think the bird watches. Us. Just to show

how slow. We move. You are eating again. The same.
          Blossoms birds lick. Pluck them from green stems.
Before rain comes. Until we are spider deep. Creak along waxed floors.

                    Imagine our wings opening. Closing behind us.
Arched points. Reach. Predictable movement. We wrap ourselves.
          Moth-thin fabric. Smooth petals. Press the seams.

Still. Spinning nocturnes with our fingernails. Spun. Spin. Still. You.
                    In empty songs. Nests of. Flight pretends itself
over us. Again. Our wings, like broom bristles. You hold up. A mirror.

          The reflection hums. Evergreen. Bleeds. Flying feels
like. Nothing. Your arms bend around my torso. Lie on your back.
                    Listen. Crackle of straw. Pluck pieces of grass.

From teeth. Your tongue a stem against my neck. These things
          we collect. Sit on hand-carved shelves. On dogwood.
Everything looks the same. But the movement of your back. June

                    crawls along skin. This Scuttle. Shuffle. Remember.
Flowers always bloom again. In morning sun, with dew.

Neon Lights, Aphrodisiac

Neon lights break in our hands
spilling colors we have always
imagined into our fingerprints,
into creases and lines of our palms,
glass cutting in long seams
mixing with our saliva and blood.
You lick at it with a dark fury,
look up at me with canary yellow
staining your upper lip.
My hands remain violet, edging
toward black, Vodka cream
shadowed hands that are used
to covering parts of your body
or mine. We are always
stealing light from street lamps,
pulling cords of pink or yellow
from buildings and homes to wrap
around our arms, coiling
a stretch of luminosity into skin.
When it becomes an addiction
we know it – we pull threads
from a battery-free flashlight,
spend our afternoons
taking turns to wind it up.
Our arms are sore, heavy
with the twine of light, your fingernails
glow in radioactive spurts,
fluttering off and on and off
like the lights of the city.

We haven't taken to standing
        in shadows yet, only because
we don't want to feel them
        drape over us in dark licks.

For Son

fingers rake skin
along the body I have nursed
kneed it like dirt, a thigh
a shoulder, until no longer
skin at all, but embroidery
          a body I have
nursed to imagine death-seams
put my face against
to find breath, a body
I have skin stitched beneath
my fingers splinter we breathe
together, leave together
breath sewing air between us
a hollowing out, a break
in the body's knowing
what I have in my hands
I have unuttered hems
these frozen buttons, novas
exploding on the floor
what I have left in another's
hands thread suture the aching

Essay on Co-Dependency

1. Introduction:

It began with a scent.
Something like knives
sharpened, slick, but not
paring knives. Those
were too small. I'm talking
butcher knives. The kind
in scary movies. The kind
you find the most blood on,
a knife that sounds like it sings
a silver lullaby when you flick
it through the air. This scent
of sliced azalea petals hidden
between the pages.

2. Body

Say there are needles hidden
in the cuffs of your sleeves.
Say my arm bleeds with prisms.
Say we fall asleep at the same time,
that our dreams overlap like languages.
Say my nipples are soft
and pink like begonias, that you
remember what they look like
when you see the blurred ovals
of my eyes. Say it. Say it with
color. Say that
there is an answer
to my childish question:

Why is the sky so blue so gray?
Say that blue is the color
of lakes we will run to,
the color of roundness
and movement,
gray like our photos
aging in frames.

3. Conclusion:

My anger drips
with myself – the colors
of my hand, my freckles.
Fingernail polish chips
and snags, cuts. Everything
is your face and synapse. Silver,
lacking body. Voices connect
and pull apart slowly, skins
deleting skins. Red beneath.
No pink. Colors un-swarming,
rewinding. It reminds me
            how we move
from one side of the bed
to another, from there to there.
Your hands. My audacity.
Yet, I am not speaking
concretely enough. I need
proof, like leaves crackling
beneath feet, or wet towels
molding on the bathroom
floor. Your leaving
somehow not enough.

Love Letter Number 137

Don't tell me the aching shoulders
are from vertigo, as if my edges
lined in cellophane, waver in light,
each pulse of my finger a lost trinket.
You press your palms together
and open them like a locket,
but whose face lingers there
in the skin, in the lines, the fingerprints?

Sometimes I dream you into the water
and you are swimming above me
like a sky. And it's worth the wait,
worth the watch and bleed of numb.

Other times, I find you broken on sidewalks,
only pieces of you scattered –
a lung here, fingernail clippings here,
and I pick up each piece imagining
where the threads would go,
what kind of stitch it would take
to re-see you whole.

My breath aches of silence,
and between each inhale and exhale
I understand what it is to be lost
between lips. You shape
into a wing. Then a boat.
I will wait to watch you skim
across smooth waters,
your oars reaching and digging,
as if you push toward sky,
toward color, toward open mouth.

When Want Becomes Salt

Try to open this casket
with a burning clam shell,
Listen for the scrape
of husk and copper,
incisions for each claw
and nick on the smooth
pearl-blue lid. Remember:
a boat in a frame
            does not sway,
no matter how blue
and dark the waves
swoop up, clinging
in strokes to a wet page.
Salt poured onto glass
cuts, each grain
a place on your tongue.
Tell me what it's like
to hold the sea floor
in your mouth, to release
it like a polished stone
into someone's palm.
When want becomes salt
and grit, the intimacy
            is concrete.
Your hair is not an anemone,
these wet curls shaping
down your back, electric
eels, reaching. Open
the casket and you'd find
velvet lining, a silk pillow,

breathing contours,
more mimicry of pearl,
sheer linens and twills
seaweed tailored, panels
lined in coral, weeping
color. Where is the red
cherry? The birch
or mahogany? Wet
with the sea
            and its mood,
its hard breathing?
You dream it so hard
it dreams away.

Self-Portrait as Mortician

When my cousin was young, she broke
into a window of a neighbor's home
to steal a bracelet she had noticed
on a table, and instead found the woman

dead on her bed, her limbs grey-blue
and bruised, her mouth open in an
unuttered vowel. Surprise or ache,
my cousin always urged both.

What she remembered were the green
eyes, the fingers pointing to the floor,
the smell of the body, like it had soaked
in sewer water and lilacs, the woman's

night gown lifted to her chest,
her soft belly tugged over the elastic
of her panties, her breasts uncovered,
slack with gravity. The first woman

my cousin ever saw naked had died
of an asthma attack before turning
out the light for bed. Years later,
my cousin works in a mortuary,

helping families move through grief
and I still can't stop gazing at the dead
bodies. At every funeral I look for it -
a color, a breath, a nudge. The smell
my cousin described, movement. But,

there are no sweet smells or mixtures
or jolts of casket wheels. I can see
myself in the waxed surfaces,

looking. Just a squint, wishing I could
knead the skin of these bodies with
my own hands, to reshape them,
to pull an arm up and to lift a leg,

to sit them into rocking chairs,
help them recline on soft couches,
imagining my cousin must forget
to wear her rubber gloves

as she undresses each body,
wipes it down, remolds the wounds,
hides the bruises, imagining
the dead could somehow become

animated once more, if only
we'd keep massaging, touching,
if only we'd just stop looking.

Mary Stone Dockery is the author of two chapbooks, *Aching Buttons* (Dancing Girl Press) and *Blink Finch* (Kattywompus Press), forthcoming in 2012. Her poetry and prose has appeared in many fine journals and has been nominated for a Pushcart Prize. She earned her BA from Missouri Western State University and will soon earn her MFA from the University of Kansas. She is the co-founding editor of *Stone Highway Review* in addition to reading for *Echo Ink Review*, *A Cappella Zoo*, and *Gemini Magazine*. Currently, she lives in Lawrence, Kansas, with her husband and their toy poodle, Rufio. This is her first book.

photo by Dustin Dockery and Jana Tigchelaar

www.ingramcontent.com/pod-product-compliance
Lightning Source LLC
LaVergne TN
LVHW051016080826
845145LV00009B/2651